PR

CONFIDENTIAL

Nik,

Enjoy!

PR CONFIDENTIAL

Unlocking the Secrets to Creating a Powerful Public Image

AMANDA PROSCIA
Foreword by Ethan Rasiel

Jarrowchase Media
New York

PR Confidential
Copyright © 2023 Amanda Proscia
Jarrowchase Media

All rights reserved. No part of this book may be reproduced or transmitted in any form, or by any means, electronic or mechanical, without written permission of the copyright owner, except for the inclusion of quotations in a review. For permissions to quote, or for bulk orders, please contact amandap@lightspeedpr.com.

Although we have made every attempt to verify the accuracy and veracity of the information contained in this book, neither the author nor the publisher assumes responsibility for any omissions, errors, or alternative interpretations of the subject matter covered.

Printed in the United States of America.

ISBN 979-8-9887202-0-1 (ebook)
ISBN 979-8-9887202-1-8 (paperback)
ISBN 979-8-9887202-2-5 (audiobook)

Book design: Clarity Designworks

CONTENTS

FOREWORD.................................... vii
INTRODUCTION................................. 1

CHAPTER 01: START HERE 5
- Everyone is telling me I should do PR, but I don't know what it is.
- We're doing marketing and advertising, so I guess we're all set.
- I've heard everything and I'm ready to start!

CHAPTER 2: ASSEMBLE PARTS..................... 13
- Maybe I need to better understand PR first.
- Everyone I know is excited about my business, so I've done my research.
- We're building on success in another market.
- The question of competition.
- What is a Marketing Plan?

CHAPTER 3: CONNECT MICROPHONE 29
- Marketing, advertising, PR and sales…do I really need all of these?
- What do you mean by earned media?
- Hang on, your job is getting reporters to write about my company? How?
- Is earned media more than just news coverage?

CHAPTER 4: TESTING...TESTING. PLEASE RESPOND . . 41
- How can I be sure the right people will see my news coverage?
- Why don't we just target the world's biggest news outlets?
- Can PR help with a crisis?
- Why wouldn't I just pay to get my content placed?

CHAPTER 5: FINE-TUNING 55
- PR can fix things after a campaign has started?
- What if our target audience was wrong?
- My business is complicated, how can PR help us?
- How will I know it worked?

CHAPTER 6: BUYING YOUR SYSTEM 63
- PR can be expensive. Will I get enough results to justify the price?
- I have someone on my team with PR experience, can I give the work to them?
- C'mon, anyone can write a press release.

CHAPTER 7: OPTIMIZING YOUR SYSTEM 69
- I hired a PR team, my work is done, right?
- I know the company is ready for PR, let's just get started.
- There's a lot we want PR to achieve this quarter.

CHAPTER 8: ENJOYING YOUR SYSTEM 75
- I followed your advice, what can I expect now?
- Is it all really worth it?

ENDNOTES 81
PUBLIC RELATIONS GLOSSARY OF TERMS 83
PUBLIC RELATIONS ACRONYMS 89
ABOUT THE AUTHOR 91

FOREWORD

by Ethan Rasiel
Co-founder, Lightspeed PR/M

I hate to say it, but the PR industry has a PR problem.

That's because there are too many PR pros who... aren't. In fact, they are PR amateurs. So many brands have been burned by PR people who over-promised and under-delivered that the whole industry has a black eye that never quite goes away.

Back in 2013, I tried to do my part to fix this. I had just left my position as director of communications at Samsung, after almost 15 years at PR behemoth Edelman Worldwide, and thought it might be time to create a new type of PR firm. One that prioritized transparency, accountability, and impactful results.

I *could* have tried to do it myself. Solopreneur, right? Plenty of PR agencies started with one person.

But I had a better idea.

Instead, I asked Amanda—the author of the book you're about to read—to join me as co-founder of Lightspeed PR. I'd known Amanda for many years as a savvy marketer with the uncanny ability to cut through BS in an instant. It just so happened we both were looking for our next opportunity at the same time. Sometimes, stars really do align.

A decade later, what is now known as Lightspeed PR & Marketing has cutting-edge clients all over the world and we have a shelf of PR award trophies. We've attracted some of the most talented PR people to make it happen. But it all started when Amanda agreed to jump to Lightspeed.

Amanda has many roles at Lightspeed, one of which is overseeing the messaging workshops for all our clients. These sessions—we call them Messaging at Lightspeed—are half brainstorming, half strategic development, and fully exhilarating. We build a narrative in real time that forms the basis of everything we do from that point forward.

A few years ago, during one of these sessions, several C-level execs from the client's team couldn't seem to agree on what their product actually did or who their ideal customers were. After 15 wasted minutes, Amanda jumped in and said, "Let me try it this way. When you are at a party and someone asks what you do, what do you tell them?" Suddenly, the mood changed, and the executive team understood what we needed. We were on our way.

As a result of the messaging we created that day, that start-up enjoyed global media attention and was later acquired by a Fortune 500 company. If someone at a party asks any of those execs to recommend a PR agency, we know how they will answer that question too.

I'm so glad you decided to read this book, and that Amanda decided to write it. She knows how to succeed, and just as important, how to learn from failure so we get it right next time. By the time you finish reading this book, you'll know those secrets too.

Use those secrets wisely—to become a better marketer or PR person. We need more of both.

—Ethan Rasiel

INTRODUCTION

During my more than 30 years of working in public relations, I've learned an uncomfortable truth: no one knows what public relations is.

There are many reasons for this. Certainly, I can blame the (very few) movies and television shows that portray PR in a vague—or worse—highly exaggerated way. For example, *Our Brand Is Crisis, Wag the Dog,* and *Scandal* present only a narrow version of what happens in political PR. And the PR done on *Sex and the City* and *Flack* is so far removed from reality that it's barely recognizable to those of us in the industry.

I do have to admit, though, that the biggest reason public relations is misunderstood is because, well…that's our job. The whole point of hiring a PR team is so they can operate from behind the scenes. Unlike advertising, our work is never displayed on a billboard, or splashed on TV. We stand in the shadows, refining messages and finding the right opportunities to change perceptions, all with deliberate, subtle moves. Which means, of course, that if we're doing our work right, no one will ever know we were there.

Unfortunately, those clandestine habits have a negative tradeoff. Not only does my own family have no idea what I do for a living, neither do many of the people whose businesses would benefit from public relations.

That's what this book hopes to remedy. In the following pages I provide unfettered access to all things PR, learned through countless hours on the job. It's an unflinching, never-said-but-often-thought, real view into what public relations professionals are actually thinking.

Sharing those thoughts is the point. Honestly, it's overdue. The answers to the questions posed in these pages are what we PR folk want everyone we work with, and everyone we know, to understand about what we do. Here's why: because they are good questions.

I mean it. Even though the anonymous letters in the chapters that follow may sound exaggerated or woefully uninformed, they're pretty accurate. Maybe you've had similar thoughts. I can tell you that these are the questions I hear every day from my clients and partners at Lightspeed PR/M.

And right here I'll start telling you the truth: We love it when people ask us these questions. Because it gives us a chance to accelerate their understanding of what we're doing. That goes a long way toward reaching our common goal of great PR results.

Unfortunately, too often that doesn't happen. The right questions go unasked, or mistaken assumptions lead to avoidable mistakes and opportunities missed.

Enough of that. Here you'll find not only the rules of the game, but every card on the table, face-up—along with the friendly banter that makes you glad you decided to play.

Use this book to learn more about public relations, or to have your questions answered before starting a PR program. If you are currently doing PR work, thinking about managing it within your own team, or you have hired a partner to handle it for you, the answers here will come in handy for you too. Make sure to use the Glossary at the end of the book. It's a cheat sheet to the endless PR terms and acronyms that pop up every day in our work.

Throughout the book are additional free resources that will give you a better understanding of the topics covered in each chapter. Those are housed on my website: lightspeedpr.com/resources and available for download.

Finally, you'll quickly notice that the book is written in letter form, with me answering the types of questions I've been hearing throughout my 30-year career. This format should make it easier for you to find exactly the information you're looking for. Also, writing it that way was a lot of fun.

So please, enjoy this unfiltered view of a too-often misunderstood profession. You can jump around to specific questions or start at the beginning and let me share the many right, wrong, and downright absurd ways I've seen PR done over the years. I hope it will be instructive. I promise it will be entertaining.

CHAPTER **01**

START HERE

 Dear PR Pro:

Everyone is telling me I should do public relations. Here's the problem: I don't know what it is, how to do it, or why I should bother. My team is nervous to take on work they've never done before and my business partner says that no one understands PR, so it can't possibly be useful. Can you help?

—STALLED AND CONFUSED

Dear Stalled and Confused:

Here's the good news: understanding public relations is easier than most people realize.

Think about it as a simple question: How do you want something to be perceived? Maybe you already know. Great, you're well on your way, and adding PR will help a lot. If you aren't sure of the answer, or if you're still struggling to define the way you want your business, product, or service to be perceived, that's all the more reason to start with PR.

When done right, public relations will help answer the question of perception, then work to make that perception a reality.

Still unsure about how it might apply to your business? Keep in mind the many, many applications of PR. It is used to reach consumers, governments, investors, partners, and influencers, to name a few. Also, remember that it can be as big or as small as you need. PR often happens on a massive scale, such as when a global business wants to reach billions of people. But public relations is also used in a more limited way, such as promoting a single product or person. Ultimately, no matter how it's applied, the end goal of public relations is always the same—creating and managing the right kind of awareness.

> "If I was down to my last dollar, I'd spend it on public relations."
> —Bill Gates, Microsoft co-founder

Why should you bother? There are a lot of good reasons. I'll get to all of them, I promise. For now, I'll quote billionaire and Microsoft co-founder, Bill Gates, who famously said: "If I was down to my last dollar, I'd spend it on public relations."

 Dear PR Pro:

Okay, so public relations is about generating awareness—that makes sense. I already have someone doing marketing and we're planning an advertising campaign. I guess we're all set!

—NO MORE QUESTIONS

Dear No More Questions:

Hang on there! It's great you're thinking about marketing and advertising. While those are related to PR, they are not all the same thing. Do you remember that first question I asked—how do you want something to be perceived? That's the key word, *perceived*.

Marketing and advertising are useful ways to *tell* people what to think. I'm sure you know what I mean: We all see ads every day, and when we do, we know that they were purchased to deliver a specific message. Ads are carefully crafted to reach exactly the right people, in exactly the right place. In other words, ads tell us what to think.

PR works differently. It *earns* people's opinions and, hopefully, their trust.

Here's a quick exercise to show you what this means. Think of a business other than your own. It could be famous and well-known, or small and local. Maybe it's a competitor to your company, or just one that you happen to follow. Got one? Okay, the next step is to consider the opinion you have about that business.

Now try to remember how you formed that opinion. Maybe you read an article about their products or services, or heard their CEO give an interview or a speech. You might say it wasn't just one thing you read or saw; you're familiar with their position on prominent issues, or even how they handled a crisis.

All of that is PR. And the business you're thinking about probably worked very hard to manage it carefully.

Still unclear? Then let's imagine I'm having a conversation with someone, and they ask me what I do. "Public relations," I'd answer. Typically, the person will say that they're familiar with it, and mention some PR work they've seen. This happens a lot. That's when I nod politely and listen to one or two examples…of advertising.

"I really liked that Super Bowl commercial," they'll say. "Then I saw a big billboard about the same thing. I remember that everyone was talking about it for a while."

When I tell them that those things aren't, in fact, public relations, the conversation gets murkier. So, I share a few examples of PR—campaigns like the Purple M&M, Barbie's "You Can Be Anything," the Breast Cancer Pink Ribbon, and the BBC's *Peaky Blinders* Fan Art.

"Oh-kay," the other person answers. "I remember all of those things." Then their face crumples in confusion. "How are those PR?"

"Those are all examples of campaigns that focused on shifting perceptions, then moved people to take action," I answer, fully aware that this isn't helping much.

A better way to understand it is with a story.

Small Business Saturday

For a number of years, I was part of the Corporate Affairs and Communications team at American Express. My time there happened to coincide with the conception and launch of a now-famous public relations initiative: Small Business Saturday. While I had nothing to do with this wonderful campaign, I did have the privilege of knowing the people who developed it, particularly Tom Sclafani, who was the architect of the original concept. Small Business Saturday, or SBS, is a great example of PR done well.

Remember my unhelpful explanation from earlier? I'm going to bring it up again here too, because SBS started by shifting perceptions. In the wake of the Great Recession in 2010, small businesses needed support more than ever. American Express wanted to encourage shoppers—especially holiday shoppers—to consider small, local retailers whose businesses depended on them more than the larger stores did.

Through the campaign, the team at American Express not only highlighted the benefits of shopping small, they also reminded consumers that their spending choices matter to their local communities. This awareness sparked a change, and Small Business Saturday has become a familiar part of every holiday season. On the Saturday after Thanksgiving, American consumers are reminded to think about where they do their shopping and, more and more often, they choose a small retailer.

As for the second part of my line, you might be wondering how that awareness moved people to take action. According to the National Retail Federation, 51 million shoppers participated in Small Business Saturday in 2021, with 71 percent indicating they were shopping specifically for Small Business Saturday.[1] And according to American Express, U.S. shoppers spent over $20 billion on Small Business Saturday in 2021.[2]

The campaign achieved what it had set out to do: SBS first shifted perceptions, helping consumers understand the importance of shopping small. Then it moved them to take action by choosing a small retailer over a large one.

 Dear PR Pro:

In your earlier answer, you said PR earns people's opinions and gains their trust. How can you be sure about that?

—I DON'T BELIEVE YOU

Dear I Don't Believe You:

That's good, healthy skepticism you have there. I encourage you to consider how advertising can be seen differently than a news story. But in case that's not enough to convince you, a 2019 study conducted by the Institute for Public Relations proved that earned media is more credible than information from other sources, including advertising.

In the study, participants of various age groups were asked to assess the credibility of those sources when thinking about a consumer purchase. It revealed that:

> The greatest percentage of participants [...] found the earned media story the most credible among the sources provided. When examining a message appearing in an

earned media story, people seek out and pay attention to cues such as the independence of the journalist writing the story, whether the story is balanced in its coverage, the credentials of the journalist, and the prestige of the media outlet where the story appeared.

Advertising certainly has a key role to play. And the study proved that as well, reporting:

People believe that advertisements are a necessary component of the promotional mix to build awareness. People recognize that the information contained in an advertisement may be somewhat biased because the company paid for it.

Basically, the study's authors proved what those of us in PR have always known: people trust what is reported in the news more than the information they know was paid for.

For more on this, download the free **Understanding PR and Advertising** resource which can be found at lightspeedpr.com/resources. It's a useful checklist to better understand the components of PR and advertising while also assessing which ones you need.

 Dear PR Pro:

Okay, you've convinced me, let's get started!

—READY TO GO

Dear Ready to Go:

Love the enthusiasm! But first I should caution you that there is more to know before you make that decision. As I said earlier, there are many ways to do PR. Better yet, there are a lot of good reasons to do it.

Public relations can be a valuable part of any marketing strategy and has even been proven to deliver higher returns on investment than other promotional efforts.

But while it can be very effective, there are just as many (if not more) ways to do PR badly. Business leaders call my agency all the time saying they're ready to start a program. Too often we end up taking a big step back to help them both identify and build foundational pieces first. The things that will be necessary to make it work.

Honestly, it would have been better if they'd simply delayed calling us.

Before starting public relations, every business needs to answer basic questions first. Those might include: What is the business hoping to achieve? Who is their target market? And is their model structured correctly to meet their goals?

Of course, I've seen other potential clients who have all the right planning in place, and still are not ready: they need more financing, haven't built the right team, there's an unaddressed flaw in their product or service, or they haven't gotten the company's leadership on board with communicating to the public. All those problems can result in a PR failure too.

That's not to say the issues can't be fixed. Usually, they can. They are just indications that the business isn't quite ready yet.

Now, I'm going to pause for a warning. If you are one of the many people who prefer to be mystified by PR and how it's done, you might want to stop here. Close the book and go right back to comfortably believing that public relations is actually advertising, or that understanding it better is too much of a bother. This is a guilt-free offer since, honestly, it's the attitude of most people I know—including my friends and family.

If, however, you really want a look behind the PR curtain to see all its gritty details—ones that will help you both understand what it is, and how to use it well—then let's get into Chapter 2.

> For more on this, download the free **Understanding PR and Advertising** resource which can be found at lightspeedpr.com/resources. It's a useful checklist to better understand the components of PR and advertising while also assessing which ones you need.

CHAPTER **02**

ASSEMBLE PARTS

 Dear PR Pro:
Okay, you have my attention. I really do want to know about PR, and especially if it's too soon for my company to start doing it.
—GETTING NERVOUS

Dear Getting Nervous:
Timing is a great place to start. As I said earlier, PR is a piece of a larger marketing strategy. In other words, doing public relations in a way that will achieve your goals means building it as a part of a marketing plan. With a good plan in place, it's much easier to determine the right time to start your PR efforts.

To make things easier to understand, I'll share another story. This one isn't as famous, or as positive, as the Small Business Saturday one, so I'm going to leave out a few details.

Once upon a time my team worked with a business that convinced us they were ready for a PR partnership. They had many of the right building blocks in place, even as a start-up technology company.

First, and most essentially, they had a solid Mission Statement that clearly communicated why they were in business. For this company, that mission was creating a new technology that would work as an add-on to other consumer tech often found in American homes. Their system would protect users' privacy whenever they used that other tech.

In addition to a product concept, this company had established a lot of other foundational things too. They had plenty of funding, an excellent team, technology that worked well, and even had the secured patents and licensing they needed to go to market.

Finally, they had the answer to a key question we ask before starting any PR program: What problem is this solving?

With all those pieces in place, they came to us ready to deploy our team to generate the kind of awareness that drives people to take action. In this case, "action" meant getting customers to purchase their product.

Sounds like a smash hit, right? Read on.

My team jumped in with a winning promotions strategy. We developed press messaging and a target outreach list, secured booths at high-profile industry events, and even weighed in on their product design, naming, and social media initiatives.

Those efforts worked, too. The new product earned a lot of interest from influential media who wanted to try it out, learn about its features, and talk to company leaders. More good news, right?

Unfortunately, no.

It turned out that, despite having come to us with a lot of the planning done, they still had not answered three essential marketing questions:

1. Is the problem big enough to justify the solution? In other words, does the product meet the 40 percent rule: Would at least 40 percent of customers say they'd be very disappointed if they no longer had access to the product?

2. Are there enough people who want to solve the problem to create the necessary demand for the product?

3. Does the price match what people are willing to pay to have the solution?

In the case of this business, terribly, all three answers were "no." Despite being clear on the problem their product solved, they never considered whether enough people wanted to solve it or were willing to pay to solve it.

Even worse, the media attention we earned only served to highlight these issues. Reporters kept focusing on the fact that the technology was priced too high. Several went so far as to interview potential users, getting feedback that uncovered an insurmountable problem: consumers were not as concerned about privacy as my client assumed they would be.

In the end, these were fatal flaws. Because the product did not solve a big enough problem, for enough people feeling the problem, and it was at a price point that was too high, the product had barely entered the market before it failed.

From a public relations perspective, my team had done everything we were hired to do. Unfortunately, even good PR could not fix the elemental marketing issues that should have been addressed long before anyone from the company called us.

As we wrapped up the project, everyone involved knew that the business had lost a great deal of time and money by pursuing the wrong product. Even worse, the client team realized that if they'd asked the right questions at the start, they could have pivoted to another solution that was better positioned for success.

Dear PR Pro:

I hear you, and that story was chilling, but I've done my market research: I've asked everyone I know if they would want to buy my product, and every time the answer is "yes." They all love it!

—I AM MY MARKET

Dear I Am...,

Okay, I'll admit it, your signature line troubled me so much I couldn't repeat it. Although the truth is, you may be right. It's entirely possible that the answers you're getting from within your own circle are a good indicator of market need.

Then again, you may be wrong.

I can promise you that the business in the story I just shared also asked everyone they knew about their product. They told us frequently how excited their friends and family were for this to be available for purchase.

In fact, prospective clients often tell us that their Mission Statement is: *This Thing Is So Cool*. And the problem it's solving is: *Who cares? It's so cool everyone will want it!*

Maybe everyone will. Wouldn't you rather be sure?

Here's a memorable way to think about this dilemma: ask a very old question, one that originated in the 1920s during the vaudeville era in the United States:

Will it play in Peoria?

Not familiar with that one? I'll give you a little background. First of all, no one knows for sure how this phrase got its start. What is known, however, is that "Will it play in Peoria?" was popularized by Groucho Marx, and soon became an entertainer's shorthand for determining whether an act would be a success across the country. Asking "Will it play in Peoria" meant stopping to think about whether the show would appeal to audiences across a range of geographies, demographics, and other important factors.

It wasn't just a punchline used by comics, either. The phrase had genuine meaning, built around the fact that the population mix of Peoria, Illinois, was a good representation of the rest of the country. For many decades Peoria "closely reflected the diversity of the United States population in terms of race, income, age, rural and business interests, educational background and other key criteria," according to *Peoria Magazine*.[3]

In the following years, the significance of Peoria as a test market began to extend beyond entertainment, making the phrase even more enduring. Not only was Peoria often the first stop on a performer's tour, but in the 1960s and 1970s major brands like Pampers, McDonald's, and Coca-Cola all used the city to test new products. Politicians knew Peoria's advantages too. John Ehrlichman, White House Counsel and Assistant to President Richard Nixon, was quoted as saying, "In some conversation or another in the White House, I said, 'How is this going to play in Peoria?' meaning how is the average American going to react to this?"

Although Peoria is no longer the mainstay test market, keep this old phrase in mind when thinking about your product's potential. I hope its origin and long-running use by prominent entertainers, business leaders and politicians convince you to stop and think beyond a quick survey of friends and family. To be more certain of success, you'll need more evidence of a real opportunity in the market.

Still don't believe me? Then maybe another phrase from the vaudeville era will help make the point. The same *Peoria Magazine* articles states that "'It Bombed in Peoria' had recognizable meaning from one coast to the other." The article explains that "Bill Adams asserted in a 1989 Journal Star column that if a show did 'bomb in Peoria,' one of several things happened: 'The production was either rewritten, recast or otherwise improved, or it was canceled altogether.'"

If your product or service needs significant changes, you will want to know it—preferably before spending time and money on something that might not have the far-reaching appeal necessary to be a success. Before starting, consider whether it will play in Peoria.

 Dear PR Pro:

While I will never think of Peoria the same way again, I have something even better. My business is built on existing success in a foreign market. Now we just need to bring it to the U.S., right?

—IT'S ONLY TOO SIMPLE

Dear It's Only Too Simple:

Oh, if only it were that simple. Sadly, I have seen far too many examples of companies that failed to repeat their overseas success in a new market. In reality, the rules of starting in another geographic region are much the same as starting out overall. You have to conduct market research to be sure that the population in the new country has as much interest in your products or services as elsewhere in the world.

To illustrate this point, I will remind you of none other than David Hasselhoff. As you probably know, "the Hoff" is the renowned star of TV's *Knight Rider* and *Baywatch*, and a multi-platinum recording artist.

If you're repeating that last detail and wondering why I would tell you something that's so absurdly untrue, you've just realized why I'm bringing up David Hasselhoff. It *is* true, with one qualifier—his music is only popular in Europe. Very, very popular. Hasselhoff has produced 14 studio albums and several compilation albums, most of which have charted in European markets (particularly Germany). However, his musical achievements have never been repeated—or even widely known—in the United States.

Maybe you're remembering Norm MacDonald's recurring joke from his time hosting Weekend Update on *Saturday Night Live*, "which once again proves my old theory that Germans love David Hasselhoff." That joke landed every time because Americans struggle to understand the TV star's overwhelming popularity in other regions. And while Hasselhoff celebrated his 70th birthday in 2022 with the launch of yet another album, *Party Your Hasselhoff*, the much-anticipated tour to support the album included zero U.S. cities.

This brings me back to that reality I mentioned earlier. Some things that are enormously popular in one market fail to find any success in another one. Start from the beginning and ask the right questions to make sure a new region will be a fit for you.

 Dear PR Pro:

I will resist the urge to buy *Party Your Hasselhoff*—for now. I have my Mission Statement, a clear understanding of the problem we're solving, and the research to prove that people in my target market will be interested. I'm finally ready to go now, right?

—CHECK THE LIST

Dear Check the List:

Well…almost. There's another big problem we haven't probed yet: Why will people want this solution from *you*? The question of competition is always a tough one, but it's just as necessary, and it requires careful research.

Many businesses over the years have assured me they know who their competition is, and what those companies are doing. Sometimes they are right. A lot of times, they're wrong. A good PR team will always want to know who else is competing for the same customers. Over the years, I've heard answers like: "Yeah, those guys are doing something similar, but it's not exactly the same as ours." Or worse: "What we have is totally unique. There is no competition."

Those answers always trigger flashing red lights in my head: Warning! Be alert for trouble up ahead!

This isn't because the answers aren't true—sometimes they are. Almost always, however, they are a sign that a business hasn't done enough research. Part of any good marketing plan will be to establish a clear point of differentiation. In other words, why will someone choose your offering over anyone else's? This is also known as a company's competitive advantage. Before you can start public relations, your team will have to know why your product or service is different, or better, than whatever already exists.

To make this clearer, I'll share another story.

Years ago, a company came to Lightspeed PR/M with a new technology that would make it easier for people to send small payments. It was positioned as the ideal solution for friends, street vendors, even the musician on the corner who didn't want to pass a hat. Unfortunately, the company's timing was against them. Other solutions were emerging that would do almost exactly the same thing—and those competitors had major funding. While my client's technology was different, and in some ways better, it was too late. Their target customers had already been captured by competitors and the opportunity was gone.

Keep an eye on what similar companies are doing, even ones that are just starting out. Track them through news feeds, industry updates, networking, and other methods. The more you know about your competition's business, leaders, products, team, and funding, the better positioned you'll be to develop something that customers might want more. A good marketing plan includes research into both your opportunity and competition.

 Dear PR Pro:

Just when I was starting to follow, you confused me again. What is a marketing plan?

—PLEASE EXPLAIN

Dear Please Explain:

There's a good reason I didn't go into detail about a marketing plan: I'm not a marketer. I leave that to the marketing experts on my team.

I can tell you that your plan should start with your business's Mission Statement and take into consideration key points, like what you're trying to achieve through your marketing. Those will probably include such vital factors as the people you will want to reach, the necessary budgets, goals and milestones, and even team roles.

As I've mentioned before, research is an essential part of the plan. Make sure you've learned as much as possible about your market—and just as important, where your particular business might fit—before you start. The plan will then work to keep your goals on track by organizing and managing your campaigns.

Of course, I know from working closely with them that marketing experts can provide more useful details on all of this. As a PR person, let me help you understand the ways that PR and marketing build upon each other.

Armed with good marketing, your PR team will have the necessary background to develop their plan. That could play out in a number of ways. For example, if you've identified your target market, we'll rely on your information to create lists of publications that reach those groups. Your market research will also help us devise key messaging that, ideally, highlights the points of differentiation that make you distinct from competitors.

Your marketing team should also share any issues they've uncovered. I'm sure you remember the story I told about the privacy tech that never found its market. If their marketing plan had discovered the fact that most people weren't concerned enough about privacy to purchase the product, we could have helped them segue to other uses with more potential customers.

I could easily go on, but I hope those few examples make clear just how well public relations and marketing work together. So, I'll say it again: if you want your PR to be successful, build it upon your marketing plan.

 Dear PR Pro:

I'm not sure what you mean by a marketing expert. Isn't that all just part of PR?

—CONFUSED AGAIN

Dear Confused Again:

That's a common question. Since public relations is too often misunderstood, it leads to people confusing it with other marketing disciplines. General marketing, advertising—and even sales—are frequently mistaken for PR, and that can cause a lot of problems. So, I will take a (very quick) step back to give you a sense of each discipline.

Start by picturing an umbrella. Got it? Great. The umbrella is marketing—that overarching piece. Now imagine that advertising and PR sit under the umbrella. While all three are contained in one image and related to one another, they are different disciplines. Marketing, PR, and advertising need to be considered separately.

Why do we need the umbrella in the first place? Because it contains a mix. Hang on, I'll explain. The "mix" starts with a legendary marketing expert named Neil Borden who came up with an easy way to think about everything under that umbrella.

Borden was a professor at Harvard from 1928 to 1942 and he coined the term "marketing mix" (see, I told you I would explain). That idea evolved into a simple breakdown of the main elements of marketing. Conveniently, they all start with the letter P: Product, Price, Place and Promotion.

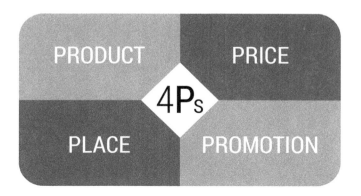

What do the **Four P's** mean?

Without getting too far off track, I'll share a little more detail on each:

Product is whatever is being sold. Maybe it really is a product, but it can also be a service, an idea or something else.

Price is pretty clear. That's the amount you will charge for whatever it is you're selling. Remember, the price should allow for a profit while still being a reasonable amount for consumers to spend.

Place is a little less obvious. It describes where you will sell your product, and it should include all the places where your customers might find it, whether that's in a store, online, through a wholesaler or elsewhere.

Promotion covers all the ways that you will promote your product in order to attract the people who might want it.

Those are the four P's. Simple enough, right? Essentially, we rely on marketing to answer all the questions about why your product exists and who might need it, how much you will charge for it, where you will sell it and—now we're getting back to classic PR: how you will promote it.

That last P is our main focus here, though the others should all be considered as part of the larger plan.

If you would like more information on the four P's, download that resource at lightspeedpr.com/resources. It's a free, downloadable chart with at-a-glance information for each P, along with questions to help you better use this essential tool.

 Dear PR Pro:

Okay, I think I see how marketing is different, but if we're focusing on promotion, isn't that advertising?

—LOST IN THE P's

Dear Lost in the P's:

You're right! Advertising is also about promotion. Just remember, as I mentioned in Chapter 1, advertisers design and place ads to tell people what to think. And again, advertising can be very effective in achieving marketing goals.

PR comes into the mix when a business wants to shift opinions. Calling back to Chapter 1 again, PR manages how people perceive something.

Quite often, advertising and PR work together so that a business can benefit from both sides. There are key differences, though. PR cannot look, sound, or read like an ad. As I said earlier, PR has to convince people instead of selling to them.

> "Advertising is saying you're good. PR is getting someone else to say you're good."
> —Jean-Louis Gassée, Apple Computer Executive

To make my point, I'll quote another prominent business leader, Jean-Louis Gassée, who is best known as a former executive at Apple Computer. Gassée summed up the distinction between PR and advertising very well: "Advertising is saying you're good. PR is getting someone else to say you're good."

 ### Dear PR Pro:

Marketing, Advertising, Public Relations. It's all starting to sound too complicated. Can't I just hire a PR firm and let them figure out all of these details?

—ONE AND DONE

Dear One and Done:

Sure you can, but it's a big gamble. Since PR is a part of marketing, it's hard to be successful without a larger plan in place.

 **Dear PR Pro:**
But what if I—

Hang on. I think I can make this clearer through an exaggerated analogy. Stay with me for a minute.

Let's say you want to build a house. As most people know, houses start from plans. Building one involves hiring skilled workers to do things like construction, electrical, plumbing, etc. Now imagine we decide to build that house *without* a plan. Instead, we just hire the plumber. After all, a plumber would work with all of those other experts. Surely that person can just do everything on their own. Seems like a safe assumption, except…what will our house look like?

No doubt we'll have great plumbing. A few other parts might be okay too. Overall, though, it's hard to believe that anyone would want to live there.

Of course, anything having to do with PR or marketing isn't as extreme as the plumber-house, and there are times when one element can function without a larger plan. Even then, there's always a chance the roof will fall in just when you least expect it.

Let me tell you about one of those times.

A wonderful company once hired my agency to promote a line of unique tech accessories. Their products made objects like chargers and speakers more fun to have around the house.

Once again, this company had many of the right starting pieces in place: great products, a strong team, plenty of financing, and even solid research into their ideal customers. That certainly gave us enough to work with, and right away we were successful in getting media attention for them. In fact, that coverage included positive reviews in top-tier publications, some of which exceeded the business's loftiest expectations.

Even with all of that outstanding PR work, after a few months our client called with distressing news: their products weren't selling. Only then did we discover glaring issues in their marketing: a difficult-to-use website, not enough retail partners, inconsistent pricing, little social media engagement… the list went on.

Even though they had assured us at the start that they were ready for PR, it turned out they had made the mistaken assumption that our work would accomplish everything they needed. I'm happy to say that they acted quickly to remedy their issues. In the end, we were able to help them out-sell their goals. Unfortunately, they lost a lot of potential sales from the initial coverage.

 Dear PR Pro:
You used the word "sales" a few times in your last answer. Can't I just use PR to accomplish my sales goals?
—SAFE TO ASSUME

Dear Safe to Assume:

That's another common misconception that my last story should warn you against. PR is not sales. In fact, let's update our umbrella image to include sales alongside PR and advertising, because good marketing will support this effort too. Sales is part of the marketing mix and will likely be built on those all-important P's. What's the product we're selling? What is its price tag? Where will we find our customers? And, of course, how will we promote it?

The same questions are foundational across all parts of the

MARKETING

PR • ADVERTISING • SALES

umbrella, and both teams should be aware of what each other is doing. In fact, our PR efforts will often include developing sales materials and providing news coverage to sales teams, to help them reach their customers. That still does not make them the same.

Once again, marketing, PR, advertising, and yes, sales are all related, but they have to be handled differently in order to be successful.

Want to know more? I'll give lots of details about this, and explain why it matters, in Chapter 3.

If you would like more information on the **Four P's**, download that resource at lightspeedpr.com/resources. It's a free, downloadable chart with at-a-glance information for each P, along with questions to help you better use this essential tool.

CHAPTER **03**

CONNECT MICROPHONE

 Dear PR Pro:

You're saying I need a marketing plan and marketing research. I might want to do advertising. And if I really want to sell, I have to hire a sales team? Gotta say, that seems like more than enough. Maybe my partner is right and there really is no need for PR.

—OUTTA HERE

Dear Outta Here:

It's a fair point and one to consider carefully. Ultimately, you'll decide whether PR should be a part of your strategy. Now, maybe it's time to take a step back. We've been talking for a while and covered a lot.

- We've established that PR is only one part of marketing and often depends on it for success.

- PR is not advertising, although they both work toward the same P: Promotion.

- It's also not sales, although they can be more successful when working together.

That's a lot of "nots," so it seems like a good time to dig deeper. We already discussed how PR generates awareness and action. And how our work is about convincing people to pay attention to you instead of selling to them, which is advertising.

That brings me to the next big topic: How?

Advertising is often called "paid media." Ads are messages that are bought and placed in order to tell people what to think.

PR aims to convince people or shift their perception of something. For that reason, it happens primarily through what we call "earned media." PR professionals work with existing media channels to get our clients' stories included.

Make sense?

 Dear PR Pro:

Ummmm. No, not at all. I think I'm more lost than before.

—HEAD SPINNING

Dear Head Spinning:

Your reaction is pretty common, honestly. I talk to a lot of people who have a general understanding of what PR is, but this is the part that trips them up. Maybe the best way to make things clearer is with another story.

We'll use a hypothetical business this time, which I will call Blarg, Inc. The good people at Blarg have hired us to promote their new product, which we'll call Widget. On our side, the public relations team is thrilled to hear that Blarg has done all of their marketing work before coming to us. They have a plan and plenty of research. They know all about their competition and are clear on the other three P's: Product, Price, and Place.

The Blarg team has also tested Widget extensively and they know their sales team can sell it. Now they need to get the word out using that last P: Promotion.

Let's say that Blarg has done some advertising. They purchased a traditional ad on television or maybe even something bigger, like a billboard. Blarg knows the value of digital media too, and they have posted about Widget on their social media channels and purchased digital ads in those spaces. Unfortunately, advertising isn't taking them far enough.

The leaders at Blarg know they need to generate the kind of awareness that only comes from earned media. They are certain that building that particular type of excitement for Widget will make all the difference in the success of its launch.

That means it's our turn. The PR team starts by developing a plan to attract that all-important earned media. It might include tactics like helping Blarg become a part of industry and consumer conferences, submitting them for awards, or finding opportunities for their leaders to give speeches at prominent events.

Blarg also wants to reach more defined groups, such as investors, partners, and even their own employees. Our PR plan might include company newsletters, intranets, or invitation-only informational events. All of those elements are commonly part of a PR plan, and they do qualify as earned media in that we are using non-paid channels—the ones people trust—to share information.

In our hypothetical scenario here, some (or all) of those tactics would be a part of the Blarg/Widget PR plan. However, they would not be the main focus. Since Blarg is hiring us to get the public interested in Widget, by far the most critical piece of our strategy would be earning news coverage.

That part of the program is always more complex, highly strategic, and closely managed. Here's how it works:

The PR team reaches out to news reporters we believe will be interested in writing a story about Blarg or Widget (sometimes both) and works with them to get that story written. By identifying many different reporters and story angles, we help Blarg win a variety of earned media coverage. In turn, that news will be read by the people who have the most interest in Blarg and their product, Widget.

I hope that by now you understand the benefit of earned media. If we had actually worked for Blarg, we would have reached potential customers through news instead of an ad or a sales pitch. And because a news story is generally seen as more credible than a message that's been bought, we would have been able to more positively influence people's opinions.

 Dear PR Pro:

Let me get this straight: your job is to get reporters to write news stories about my company? How the heck do you do that?

—NEWS IS NEWS

Dear News is News:

As to your first question: believe me, we hear that a lot. The simple answer is yes. Many people simply don't realize that much of the news they see reported every day was influenced by public relations.

Yes, really.

Your second question will take a little longer to answer. How do we do it? It's often not easy. But if we want to be successful, we know to start any media relations effort with a compelling narrative, or as I like to put it, Story with a capital S.

This goes back to our initial chat about perception. Story gets to the heart of how the business wants to be perceived. In fact, after getting started with a new client and learning their business objectives, Story is always our next discussion.

We spend a lot of time talking and brainstorming to uncover all the details of it. Then we work together until everyone clearly grasps how the client wants the public to understand their business, product, or service.

Sometimes the thing we're promoting already exists. In those cases, we research how people think of it now. Ultimately, our goal is to agree on how the client wants their business, product, or service to be seen in the future.

Once we have that decision made, the PR team builds the Story to make the desired perception, or shift in perception, happen.

Not entirely following? Okay, let's go back to Blarg, Inc. and their wonderful new product, Widget. We're at the point where we're developing the Story, and since it's going to be about Widget, we now have to know what it does.

I'm still making things up here, so I'm going to say it's a unique new technology that makes movie theater seats more comfortable. Cool product, right? Unfortunately, that's not enough to make a Story. We need more, which means we have to rely on a tool you know all about by now: a good marketing plan.

Remember all the pieces that go into a marketing plan? Well, this is where they become really helpful.

The PR team needs to know who we're trying to reach. Is it customers? Retail partners? Investors? Just as important is knowing who Widget's competitors are and what they are saying about their products. Maybe there's already a movie theater blanket and pillow on the market, and they both claim to make the seating experience wonderful. How is Widget better than that?

This is also when we ask our big question: What problem is Widget solving? And, of course, the crucial follow-up: Will enough people want Widget's solution instead of an existing one?

Since I invented the business and everything about them, I can say with confidence that Widget's patented comfort technology is far and away a better solution for movie theatergoers than those old blankets and pillows. This is great news for the PR team. We now have enough information to move forward and finally develop our Story.

But wait! The team at Blarg, Inc. tells us they have already done all the Story development. Their marketing team created brilliant messages that highlight all the ways Widget is different and better than the pillow and blanket products. They have even done market testing to prove that this is the right approach for reaching Widget's target customers: people who want to be more comfortable at the movies. And the team is particularly proud of their new tagline: "Don't Fidget, Widget!"

"This is great," we'll tell them, "We have no doubt those messages will be effective in reaching customers. That's what good marketing does. But there's a reason you're doing PR."

We have this conversation a lot. It draws a line under the biggest difference between marketing and public relations. For PR, it's not enough just to have a message that will be interesting to your customers. We are working to reach reporters. That means it's essential for our story to go further—it has to be newsworthy.

This is where a lot of PR initiatives fall apart. To make that leap into earned media, we have to offer something that a journalist finds interesting enough to report on.

Remember, the reason you hire a PR expert is because our teams are skilled at media relations. We know what is newsworthy and what isn't. We do it by maintaining close relationships with reporters and living on a steady diet of news.

Anyone who hires a PR team should expect them to know key facts: what's being reported on, by whom, and most critically, what will capture the interest of those journalists? With that in mind, we go out and get news coverage for our clients.

Dear PR Pro:

Okay, I guess I can believe that you get reporters to write news stories. But now you have me worried. How can I know if my business is newsworthy?

—WHOLE NEW PROBLEM

Dear Whole New Problem:

No problem! There's a straightforward way to determine if you have something newsworthy to say about your business. Remember the four P's of marketing? Well, at my agency, we rely on the *three I's*. Devised by my Lightspeed PR/M co-founder, Ethan Rasiel, it's our go-to formula for knowing if a business has something we can work with. It also tells us a lot about where we might place the story in the media, and even how to tell it.

The three I's are: Innovation, Impact and Insight. To be effective, a PR story has to fit into at least one of those categories. Let me explain each one in more detail:

Innovation

If someone comes to us with an INNOVATION story, it means they are doing something that is not just new, it's never been seen before. Often, it's an invention, or a disruption of an existing technology. It could even be a new work approach that changes the way things are done. Sometimes the story is a completely different business model that makes existing solutions obsolete. Or it could just be a novel way of doing things that's better.

With our agency's focus on technology, we work with many people who build their PR around innovation stories. To give you an example, I'll share a bit about one of my favorite clients, the Ulta-Lit Tree Company. Their patented products, Lightkeeper Pro and LED Keeper, solve a familiar problem: broken Christmas tree lights. By identifying and solving light issues, this technology definitely fits the Innovation category.

As their PR team, telling Ulta-Lit's story meant talking about this unique tool that was invented by the company's CEO, John DeCosmo. Needless to say, we had an easy time answering the question "what problem are you solving?"

Impact

Of course, we don't have to have something innovative to build great PR. Often someone comes to us with an IMPACT story, which works well too. This happens when they have done something significant enough that it changes the landscape of their business. Perhaps they helped other companies save money, or maybe their new way of doing things resulted in increased market share, or a shift in how their type of business is done. Basically, whenever a business can be credited with doing something with a significant impact, it's newsworthy.

For Ulta-Lit, the impact story involved their Lightkeeper Pro Hotline, a call-in line the company operates every holiday season. It's an indispensable resource for people who need help fixing their broken lights and has been used by hundreds of thousands of people over the years. We knew that kind of impact was absolutely newsworthy.

Insight

The last I, INSIGHT, offers a great option for companies that don't have an innovation or impact story to tell. Often referred to as Thought Leadership, developing an insight plan for PR usually involves promoting company leaders as experts. For example, we might place an executive on a news show or have them interviewed for an article. For these news opportunities, the executive will be asked to share their unique knowledge about their industry, another related story, or an emerging product or service.

Good Thought Leadership doesn't end there, though. PR teams will frequently draft full articles with the client's name as the byline—also known as ghostwriting—then have them placed in prominent publications. We'll also keep in touch with reporters working on similar news stories to ensure that our executives are tapped for comment whenever possible. After all, company leaders have accumulated expertise that's valuable for reporters when they are developing other articles. Creating an Insight plan is all about leveraging that knowledge to keep the leader—and their company—in the news.

Once again, I'll share how we did this for Ulta-Lit. Since we had the benefit of working with a CEO who was both an inventor and an expert on Christmas light issues, we knew Insight was another great way to get news coverage. We gave target media unprecedented access to Mr. DeCosmo, and reporters included him in stories as wide-ranging as recommendations on light sets and repair to observations on the year's decorating trends.

This brings me to another opportunity for earned media in the Insights category. It's what we PR folks call trendjacking. As I'm sure you're aware, the news often follows other big stories that are happening at that time. A PR team can identify where our clients fit into trending stories and get them involved as expert commentators.

For Ulta-Lit in 2020, we took advantage of the dominant news story: the Covid pandemic. That year, despite the festive holiday season, the ongoing news remained grim. We learned from our sources that reporters were ready for something more cheerful to cover.

In response, we positioned Ulta-Lit as a feel-good story to break through the bad news. It also dovetailed well with another emerging trend: since people were spending more time indoors,

Christmas decorations not only arrived earlier in the year, but became much more elaborate. The result of our trendjacking efforts was that Mr. DeCosmo became a sought-after expert throughout that holiday season.

It's good to remember, though, that the Ulta-Lit example is not typical. More often, a business fits into only one or two of the I categories instead of all three. I could share plenty of other case studies where we only used one or found ways to incorporate others as time went on.

But if you think you're ready to start PR and want to know if you have something newsworthy, start by thinking about the three I's.

To help that thinking, check out our free, downloadable worksheet on the **3 I's** at lightspeedpr.com/resources. It provides more detail about each of the categories along with questions to consider when deciding which one(s) are best for your PR program.

 Dear PR Pro:

Okay, I think I get the whole news thing. You mentioned a lot of other components too, like conferences, awards, speaking opportunities. PR is all of those things too?

—WHOLE PICTURE

Dear Whole Picture:

Yes, PR includes everything you just mentioned, and others too. As I said earlier, all of those are considered earned media because they rely on sources that aren't bought to tell our story. Earning a speaking opportunity at a conference or winning an award both indicate that someone else thinks the business's work is valuable. That type of recognition can go a long way in gaining the right kind of awareness. It's why these elements are often a central part of a PR plan that is seeking to influence the opinions of people in the public.

But it doesn't stop there. Often a business wants to shift perceptions of other groups. I've mentioned a few examples, including investors, business analysts, politicians, strategic partners, or a company's own employees. All of those groups can be reached through methods other than getting news coverage. The PR team manages those efforts as well.

We'll create a program developed specifically to speak to whichever groups are most valuable to our client.

- Sometimes we throw an event and invite our target groups.

- We might script and host informational sessions.

- We develop and disseminate newsletters to reach other specific audiences.

- Or we might leverage online channels for direct outreach (intranet sites, private groups on social media, blogs, and others).

Basically, you can rely on a PR team to do whatever it takes to reach the right people in the right way.

 Dear PR Pro:

That sounds like a lot to do. How can PR be responsible for so many different types of work?

—TIRED HEARING ABOUT IT

Dear Tired Hearing About It:

It is a lot to do and certainly can get complicated. Keep in mind that a PR team is made up of many people, all of whom bring different skills. Media experts get involved when media relations is a part of the program. They also make sure your story is the right one, and then work to get it covered.

However, depending on the focus of your PR effort, your team might include other strategists who develop the plan and overall messaging. Those people stay in touch with you on a day-to-day basis, analyze and report on results, and oversee the larger PR program, making sure it stays on track as it progresses.

Sometimes PR teams include specialized talent, such as a writer to develop content (these people are great when you have an Insight story); subject matter experts who know all about your particular work or industry; events managers; and speaking and award teams to work on behalf of a client's business. And that's just naming a few.

Of course, you'll likely also have support staff who take on such tasks as monitoring news coverage and making sure everyone on the team has everything they need to be successful.

Again, this list just scratches the surface. There's a lot more to consider before really understanding what PR is and how it's done. Want to keep going? Let's jump into Chapter 4.

> Remember to check out our free, downloadable worksheet on the **3 I's** at lightspeedpr.com/resources. It provides more detail about each of the categories along with questions to consider when deciding which one(s) are best for your PR program.

CHAPTER **04**

TESTING...TESTING. PLEASE RESPOND

 Dear PR Pro:
Getting news sounds great, but even if we get a reporter to write about my business, how can I be certain the right people will see it?
—NOT CONVINCED

Dear Not Convinced:
You have just uncovered another essential part of any public relations effort, well done! Getting this right involves a lot of steps, including research, list development, relationship building, targeted outreach, and even trial and error.

It all starts with one word: audiences.

I know that might conjure up images of people sitting in a theater or rushing the stage at a concert. For us, it's simply asking the question "Who are we trying to reach?"

As you probably guessed, this is yet another part of a marketing plan. An essential part, in fact. In PR, it takes on new meaning for exactly the reason you pointed out. We have to reach our audience through channels that we don't control, such as the news media.

How do we do that? It's a multi-layered process with an essential first step: understanding who makes up the audience.

As an example, let's go back to that concert I just mentioned and think about the people who might be there. Maybe it's happening at a massive stadium where the audience is rocking out with Taylor Swift. Or at a downtown café where people are seated at small tables to hear an acoustic guitarist. Other audiences might be enjoying a symphony with the New York Philharmonic or filling the bleachers at a middle school gymnasium for their annual choir performance.

While all of those events qualify as concerts, I think you'll agree that the people in each audience would vary widely depending on which show they are watching.

The exercise is the same for deciding who we want to reach with PR. Is our client's audience a group of devoted Swifties? Or are they women over 40 who love Vivaldi?

Too often we hear that the company's audience is "everyone." Maybe that's true, but it does make our work harder. The better we can pinpoint which segments of people we're talking to, the easier it will be to reach them. I can make this clearer by going back to our awesome made-up company, Blarg, Inc.

Since their product will be most useful for people who go to movie theaters, you could say that Blarg's "target audience" is a large and diverse group. That's because many different people enjoy going to the movies. For the most effective PR, it's wise to start with one segment of that group, which, of course, is the one most likely to be interested in our product.

Let's say that we've identified the target audience as people in their twenties and thirties who go to at least two movies per month. Why those people? Our research shows that with their frequent movie theater visits, this group understands the value of being more comfortable during that experience and is open to a product that would help.

With that decision made, we have now identified a likely group of customers for Widget. Now we have to get as detailed as possible about that audience. Since we know there are many more movie theaters in urban and suburban areas, it's likely that's where our group lives, with easy access to those movies they so love. They would also have to earn above a certain income level to afford a lot of tickets. That works well, because it also means they can probably afford our product, Widget. Now comes the big PR question: How do we reach them?

We start with research.

Target Media Research

A PR team starts by compiling a list of media publications that are seen by the target audience. Are they entrepreneurs who read business and tech magazines? Or maybe they're consumers who follow the latest trends in lifestyle or even fitness publications? We might have a client who is only interested in reaching people in a particular business segment. For them, the best media targets could be trade publications that focus on certain industries. Depending on the audience, our list building might go in many different directions.

Next, our research drills down to finding the right reporters at each of those publications. We identify the people who would be most interested in covering our story.

Finally, we audit recent news and connect with reporters in our network to leverage trending news stories.

Only then are we ready to move on to outreach.

Outreach

Armed with our lists, the team will start contacting reporters. There are several ways to do this. Sometimes we'll draft a press release announcing the client's news, but frequently we'll just send emails that contain the information we think is most interesting to each reporter.

Once we find someone who wants to cover our news, the team works closely with them to develop the story until it's ultimately published.

Now I can finally get back to your question, Still Not Convinced. At this stage we ask ourselves, "Did it work?"

Measurement

It's notoriously difficult to measure public relations, although we can watch a few key indicators. Those include things like shifts in sales of their product, traffic to their website, increases in social media engagement, and overall awareness of the business.

Another valuable report we'll give our client is on the media coverage itself. We'll gather all the news media that reported on them, and importantly, the number of people who read those publications. It won't surprise you to learn that some news goes farther than others. For example, an article in *USA Today* will be seen by more people than one published by a blogger. The bigger the news source, the more members of our target audience have been reached.

Hang on, we're still not done!

Rinse and Repeat

After all of that effort, the PR team will go back over everything that was done to uncover any other stories we think might gain more interest, or to refine ones that didn't work as well as expected. We might even add new elements, like content creation or social media. Then the whole process starts over again.

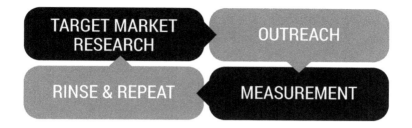

To learn about and discover your own target audiences, download the free Finding Your Audience flowchart and guide at lightspeedpr.com/resources. It will provide essential things to consider, followed by a real audience breakdown in simple (and amusing) steps.

 Dear PR Pro:

It sounds like the smartest thing to do is reach out to the world's biggest news reporters and get them to cover my story. Why don't we just do that and hit all my business goals right away?

—FAST FORWARD

Dear Fast Forward:

I agree, it would be great to do it that way, and on rare occasions we can. But most of the time, that's simply not how it works. Think about it: how often do you read an article in the *Wall Street Journal* or see a story on *Good Morning America* that's about a company you've never heard of before? Probably not very often.

The reason is simple: news builds on news. The more we can do to generate interest from the smaller, more focused news sources, the more we can build up to the bigger ones. I'll share another story from my agency's work that demonstrates this.

Lightspeed PR/M had the privilege of working with a company at the cutting-edge of medical device technology. Because of the scientific complexity of their product, the larger news outlets simply didn't have the background to properly understand the groundbreaking work being done. As a result, that type of media was hesitant to cover our client until they could be certain that everything we were claiming was true. We knew we had to start small.

We developed a plan to first engage with scientific publications and their highly trained reporters. That way we could tell the story of our client's work, while also demonstrating to mainstream news outlets that it had passed the rigors of the scientific community. Once we had that success, our team could build the news one step at a time, starting with the small, research-focused publications, and then onto larger ones. With that accomplished, we targeted health and science reporters at next-tier media, and so on.

This strategy succeeded in earning great coverage from prominent health, science, pharmaceutical, and other publications. Ultimately, we won enough validating news that we were getting stories in the *New York Observer* and the *Washington Post*.

Now, before you tell me your business isn't as intricate as something in health science, I'll stop here to remind you that the rule remains the same in most cases. When we're able to win over smaller, industry-focused publications and writers, the more success we have with larger news outlets.

 Dear PR Pro:

If we have to build small to big, won't that take a lot of time? How quickly will I see the results of my PR work?

—LET'S GET GOING

Dear Let's Get Going:
Here is yet another distinct reason why PR is different from the other disciplines under our Marketing Umbrella: PR takes time. Here's a quick review of everything we discussed that goes into effective PR:

Shifting perceptions
↓
Motivating action
↓
Developing a story
↓
Building reputation with reporters
↓
Developing news coverage, small to large
↓
Reviewing and improving
↓
Repeat all over again

As you can see, all of these steps require an investment of time, strategic planning, review, and patience. While marketing and advertising can offer short-term results, public relations should be considered a long-term investment that pays off over time. And there's good news too: that upfront investment will often return steady results. Once a business establishes its reputation and demonstrates the value of its products or services, PR can continue to build on that, creating more and more opportunities.

But since you're eager to get results, I'll give you another way to think about it. Seeing the benefits of PR can be compared to joining a gym. If you're a new gym member, it's going to take time and effort to work up to the fitness levels you want. You have to try out different exercises to learn which ones work best for you, then show up as often as possible to build muscle and endurance. Only after that work has been done will you really achieve your goals.

See the similarities?

There's another useful lesson here too: the sooner you start, the better. If you want to be in shape for summer, it's a good idea to join the gym in the spring or earlier. The same type of planning should apply to your PR program. The more time your team has at the start, the better they will be able to set you up for success.

 Dear PR Pro:

Building to results is one thing, but my business is dealing with a crisis. We've been getting terrible customer reviews after a few tech hiccups. How can PR help us before our reputation is permanently damaged?

—STILL STINGING

Dear Still Stinging:

I'm sorry you are dealing with negative press. Rest assured, your PR team can help. Initially, though, it's wise to take a step back and determine what type of response is needed.

Frequently, clients responding to bad reviews tell us the same thing you did: that it's a crisis. Fortunately, that's rarely the case. Most of the time what these situations call for is reputation management. (Believe me, this is better.)

Don't worry, I'll explain the difference: A crisis team is called in when something awful has happened because of your company. A famous example of this is the 1982 Tylenol poisoning deaths. That tragedy dominated the headlines and resulted in Johnson & Johnson, the owner of Tylenol, halting production and advertising of the product. A true crisis, the incident led to the deaths of seven people, hundreds of copycat attacks, and widespread distrust in drug manufacturers. For Tylenol, the effects were particularly devastating: the company's market share collapsed from 35 percent to eight percent.

However, because of proper crisis management, the brand recovered quickly. Through quick action, honesty with the public, and working with law enforcement to help prevent further tampering, the company ultimately received positive news coverage. That included an article in the *Washington Post* that stated, "Johnson & Johnson has effectively demonstrated how a major business ought to handle a disaster."[4]

Thankfully, crises like these don't happen often to companies. Much more frequently, they will find themselves in the same situation you're in: the subject of negative press that has to be managed. That's not to say this type of brand damage doesn't feel like a crisis to the people in the company. It certainly can. Although, as I said, it falls into the category of reputation management.

I'll share an example of this from our work at Lightspeed PR/M to illustrate how PR can be the right strategy.

At one time we worked with a tech company whose product protects computers from malware. Unfortunately, some bad actors in their history had damaged the company's reputation severely. Re-focused with a new leadership team and a much-improved product offering, our client was ready to put the past behind them with a PR effort. We knew it wasn't going to be that easy.

Online reviews and even continued media coverage still criticized the company and urged potential users to keep away. Our strategy: face the past and rebuild trust.

Through a revised PR effort that focused on coming clean with the media, owning the company's mistakes, and working hard to demonstrate its improvements, we slowly repaired their reputation. It took time, persistence, and many uncomfortable conversations with reporters. Ultimately though, the reviews began to shift from negative to positive. I'm happy to say this business is now doing well, with products that are once again trusted and relied upon.

Keep in mind, Still Stinging, that patience is the most vital piece of the plan. As in all other PR responses, rebuilding a reputation takes time. If you stick with it and trust in the process, your results can be transformative.

 Dear PR Pro:

Okay, I see the value in getting news coverage, but why should I hire a PR team? I get emails all the time offering me opportunities for press coverage.

—ISN'T THERE AN EASIER WAY

Dear Isn't There An Easier Way:

I'm not exaggerating when I tell you that we hear about those "opportunity emails" from clients every day. They forward whatever was sent to them and within seconds we recognize it as something we call "Pay to Play." Since those types of emails are becoming more common, let me take a minute to explain what they are, and importantly, what they are not.

Despite what you might read in their (many) emails, these are not real publications. Please take a second and read that again. Not. Real. The content they publish is written by hired writers who aren't reporters, and it is not respected as news. That means anything they write about you will not be seen as actual press and could, in the end, damage your reputation.

Even if nothing negative comes from working with them, it's unlikely that anything positive will result from it either. Most of these so-called publications have limited reach. That means anything you have published there will only be seen by a few people. It's rarely worth the effort.

Here are a few ways to figure out if that "great opportunity" is actually Pay to Play:

- **Are they persistent?** A real news publication will likely not reach out repeatedly.

- **What is their web presence?** Check to see if they have a template-style website with a lot of recent articles, or social media sites covered with ads. Those typically mean the publication is not legitimate.

- **What are they asking?** If they want money to write something on your behalf, that's a sure giveaway. Real reporters don't sell their work.

> - Are they persistent?
> - What is their web presence?
> - What are they asking?

The bottom line is, paying for this type of coverage will have real costs and little benefit. A PR program will take more time and effort, but the results will go much farther.

 Dear PR Pro:

I see your point and I definitely want a lot of news coverage. How many stories can my PR team guarantee?

—I WANT A SURE THING

Dear I Want a Sure Thing:

If you have a good story, and the right team, you've planned well and give everything enough time— I'll stop there. Because while those things make a difference and will more than likely lead to news coverage, the hard truth is that no PR team can ever guarantee press.

Do you remember the last conversation, and what I said about real reporters not selling their work? That's because in most of the markets where we engage the media, your PR team is dealing with a free press. Which means, of course, that they decide what news is reported on. And how it's reported. And when it's reported.

Earning press coverage has value for exactly that reason: it's earned.

Yes, we know a lot of ways to get their attention and have plenty of time-tested methods to set ourselves up for success. It's still not up to us.

That hard truth I said at the start should be kept in mind whenever doing PR with anyone. If they offer a guarantee… Well, you've been warned.

 Dear PR Pro:

I get it, no guarantees. Except when you do get coverage, it's a story you've given to a reporter. That means it can say whatever I want, right?

—LET'S TAKE CONTROL

Dear Let's Take Control:

Again, no. I'm sorry to keep disappointing you, but maybe it's time to go back to that last point about a free press. Reporters are respected because they write the news in the way they see fit. Of course, they appreciate it when PR people give them good stories and other helpful things, like executive interviews and supporting collateral. Those resources are all useful in positioning our clients in the best way possible. That's where our control ends.

Here's an example that might make it easier to understand. My agency has had the opportunity to work with many companies that develop and sell consumer electronics. Because these gadget-type products are best understood when they are experienced, we frequently send samples to reporters. Usually this works out great. The target reporter gets to play with their new tech, see it in action, and even test it for flaws. After they've evaluated the product for themselves, they will often write a review based on that experience. And because our clients make wonderful products, we generally expect that experience to be good.

Until it isn't. Even the best product isn't the right fit for everyone and when that happens, the reporter will tell the truth. Maybe it broke or had features that failed. It could be that the gadget just didn't fill a need for that particular person. Whatever the reason, the resulting news story might be less than flattering.

Of course, we try to make things better. We offer to send a new sample, give them more background on its uses, or set up time to answer additional questions. Sometimes that response is effective, and a revised article will be published. Sometimes it isn't. In the end, getting credible news stories written by reporters who share their genuine opinion is why earned media is so highly valued.

A good PR team won't stop there, though. There are lots of ways to revise, refine, and improve our efforts to get—or even extend—our success. Want to know how? Keep reading.

> To learn about and discover your own target audiences, download the free **Finding Your Audience** flowchart and guide at lightspeedpr.com/resources. It will provide essential things to consider, followed by a real audience breakdown in simple (and amusing) steps.

CHAPTER **05**

FINE-TUNING

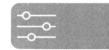

 Dear PR Pro:
You're saying that a PR team can fix things even after the campaign has started? How?

—TOO LATE

Dear Too Late:

It's never too late! The people running your PR program are watching everything closely to evaluate what is working and what isn't. This deliberate process allows them to make revisions and changes along the way. Those learnings—and revisions—often lead to better results.

Since that answer was a bit vague, let's go back to our first discussion about what PR professionals do: influence people's perceptions. And if you can remember all the way back to Chapter 3, that effort starts with Story.

As I said earlier, we spend a lot of time talking with the client about their products, services, and business objectives, with a particular focus on how they want those things to be seen. Then, along with market research, we develop the Story that we think will resonate with our target media. You remember all that, right?

Great. So, what happens if that Story doesn't work as well as we expected it to? Or it does work, but it's not as successful as it could have been? As hard as we try to get it right the first time, there are instances when our teams develop an imperfect narrative or present it in the wrong way. What then?

We change it.

Let me tell you how this worked for a tech company we represented a number of years ago. A fascinating business, this client is at the leading edge of augmented reality (AR) and virtual reality (VR). In fact, they hold hundreds of patents for the innovative AR/VR components that they've invented and produced. Given their unparalleled authority in the space, our original plan was to tell the story of their products and all the incredible things they can do. We certainly got some media interest; it just didn't go as far as we had expected. At the time, reporters were still struggling to understand the benefits of AR/VR technology. They were also aware of user resistance to these types of consumer products, making the news less interesting to their readers.

We paid attention. By gathering feedback from our media contacts and reopening Story conversations with our partners, we came to a conclusion: our issues stemmed from a lack of understanding. That meant we had to re-focus the Story to educate our audience.

That's when we turned our attention to the company's remarkable leadership, and crafted new pitches that leveraged their decades of knowledge and expertise.

In the end, this approach worked. In fact, the very same media that had rejected our original pitch started clamoring for interviews with the company's CEO and engineers. In a short time, they were being featured in many of their target publications, and were even invited to speak at industry events.

Needless to say, PR teams may use many different approaches and find ongoing creative solutions throughout a campaign. Often, client partnerships last for many years, spanning dozens of launches, announcements, and other opportunities for media outreach. For each one, the PR experts involved will look for new angles, revised story lines, additional media targets, and future narratives that can be developed and extended for ongoing success.

 Dear PR Pro:

I guess it makes sense that you can revise your story, but what if your audience was wrong too?

—NOBODY'S LISTENING

Dear Nobody's Listening:

Sure, that can happen. Despite our best planning and research, PR teams might wrongly conclude that the best audience for their client's story is the one listening to Taylor Swift, when in fact it was the one in the middle school gymnasium.

Not to worry! We can pivot here too. In the same way that we're paying attention to how the media is reacting to our story, we gather the same feedback about our strategy for the audience.

Maybe we're hearing from target reporters that they just don't have interest. Or they like the story, but don't think it will capture their readers' or viewers' attention. That's when we know it's time to find a new audience. I'll share another example to bring this to life.

For a few years, my agency had the privilege of working with a cutting-edge technology company that made virtual presence robots. If you bought one, you could send the robot to some other location and use its screen and mobility to see, hear, and move through that other place. Pretty cool, right? We thought so too. We were also certain that the technology media would be the ideal audience, thinking it would be exactly the type of news they'd want to share with their tech-savvy, early-adopter readers.

We were wrong.

While those reporters all agreed that the robots had great technology and a lot of potential for use, they didn't like that the actual product was somewhere they weren't. Instead, they believed their readers would be disappointed to own technology that they couldn't touch and interact with.

Now, I can't say we weren't surprised by this response, but we did learn from it. And pivoted. For our next round of outreach, we targeted audiences who might have less passion for the technology, but more of a need for it. That included educators, doctors, students, remote workers, even cleaning and maintenance crews. By uncovering and telling the use cases of how real people were taking advantage of what the robot could do, we captured the interest of reporters from across many categories and industries.

That brings me to another important point about audiences: many businesses have more than one. A good PR team will always look for additional angles to your story, or other ways they can engage with a range of audiences. And while they might need to start with one segment, that initial success can be the foundation for many more opportunities.

 Dear PR Pro:

It sounds like public relations is a good solution for typical problems faced by businesses. Unfortunately, we deal with lots of things that aren't typical. Just last year we had a supplier fail to deliver, we lost our Chief Marketing Officer, and we even had to shut down our manufacturing plant for a safety review. Can PR really help with those things?

—STOP THE MADNESS

Dear Stop the Madness:

In a word: yes. By working closely with you and your team, PR experts can develop responses to all the things you mentioned, and others too. The best approach is to engage with them early so they can learn as much as possible about your work, industry, partners, products, etc. If that happens at the outset, your team can be ready to handle whatever issues might come up later.

Remember that your team will also engage with your target media on an ongoing basis. They are in an ideal position to communicate what's happening within your business and manage that story as best as possible.

You mentioned that your supplier failed to deliver. I imagine that resulted in a lack of inventory, which might have led to canceled customer orders or other problems. When that happens, you can deploy PR for a two-pronged response. First, a PR team would work with you to determine what to share with the media and your customers. As an example, they might decide to explain where things went wrong, and provide a firm timeline for when operations will return to normal.

The second prong is reaching out to the right media to tell your story accurately. That might require access to your leadership, and possibly even some of your affected customers.

Which brings me to another critical point. Public relations is a collaborative effort. No matter how skilled or experienced they are, your PR team will need ongoing partnership with you, your staff, your leadership, and possibly other stakeholders in your business. This is especially true during difficult times when things are happening quickly. If you want PR to be an effective part of your solution, keep the lines of communication open.

Overall, having the right PR team in place, with essential knowledge of how your business operates and relationships with key reporters, will help you get past these difficulties more easily. Even if they are far from typical.

Dear PR Pro:

Let's say I believe you and do all these things you're recommending. How will I know that it worked?

—I WANT ANSWERS

Dear I Want Answers:

That's a great question, and one without an easy answer. Since our work is about shifting perceptions, it's not always measurable. The best way to know how well PR worked is to focus on your goals for doing it in the first place. In other words: Why did you hire a PR team?

Was it to get more sales of a product or service? In that case, take a look at your sales numbers and see if there was any increase. Maybe you wanted to attract investors, partners, or employees. Did that happen? If you're responding to negative press or community comments, how did those change or improve?

Again, I do have to emphasize that results will take time. Too often clients tell us that the first press release, sent last week, didn't deliver massive sales. That's because perception change simply doesn't happen that quickly. Keep an eye on measurement, but do not expect to see major shifts for at least a few months, sometimes longer.

Getting back to your question, let me give you an example of the results we earned for the Ulta-Lit Tree Company and their wonderful CEO, John DeCosmo (the client I mentioned earlier). In our first year working to promote their tools for fixing Christmas tree lights, we had a long list of great media results. The company went from having very little online presence to being the go-to experts on all things related to tree lights and decorations. We then wanted to answer the same question you asked: how did it work?

The team at Ulta-Lit was happy to report that our efforts led to a 35 percent increase in sales over the previous year. And since that was their goal for PR, we considered our program to be successful.

You might be looking for those types of big-picture shifts too, and you can expect your PR team to deliver reports of all the indicators they watch. Those should include measurable data like website traffic, social media engagement, search engine optimization (SEO), and other data that can be tracked and evaluated.

You should also receive reports on your media performance that include key points like the number of stories placed and the average readers or viewers of that coverage. PR folk refer to that as Media Impressions. For example, if a story appears in a newspaper that has one million readers, we would estimate your business received one million "impressions" from that story.

PR teams often report on the value of that coverage by researching how much it would cost to place an advertisement in that same news outlet. Increasingly popular is a report that shows Share of Voice (SOV). This measures the number of earned stories you received compared to a competitor. The goal with SOV is to evaluate whether you are getting more attention than other players in your industry.

Those are just a couple of examples of measurable output from PR. Of course, if your company is enjoying an overall uptick in enthusiasm about what you do, that might lead to happier employees, more industry awards, invitations for keynote speeches, meetings with better partners, or higher demand for your products and services—to name a few. And while it may be harder to measure those benefits, they are often the result of good PR.

> Get our free, downloadable **PR Measurement Guide** at lightspeedpr.com/resources. It's an indispensable reference for all the measurement tools used in PR, and how to use them for better results. The guide also includes a 12-month checklist to review any measurement tools that might be missing in your current program.

CHAPTER **06**

BUYING YOUR SYSTEM

 Dear PR Pro:

All of this sounds great, but let's be honest, PR can cost a lot of money. How do I know I'll be getting enough results to justify the price?

—R.O.I. GUY

Dear R.O.I. Guy:

As with any investment, you can never know for sure. Fortunately, there are ways to set up your partnership to deliver a good return.

The first one takes us back to our (many) earlier exchanges. I'm going to remind you again of that all-important marketing plan. In addition to all the other arguments to develop one, believe it or not, there is also a sound financial reason.

Let's consider our fictitious client Blarg, Inc. once again, and their product, Widget, which makes movie-watching more comfortable. Only this time, the folks at Blarg didn't do their marketing plan. Instead, they started PR without any research into the market opportunity for Widget. They didn't know who the competition might be and had zero understanding of their target market.

Unfortunately, PR people hear things like this a lot. We're given goals based entirely on guesses. Now, it's possible those guesses are right, and our efforts end up reaching the right people with the right messages. Too often, that's not the case. Far more frequently, we spend a great deal of time and effort only to find out that the client's assumptions were wrong. Even worse, the money they spent on PR returned little to no results. Expensive, right?

Of course, having a marketing plan is not the only way to make sure your PR investment will return as much as possible. You also need to choose the right partner. The best way to do that is to remember that all public relations people aren't the same. You might have a sister-in-law who happens to do PR, but that doesn't mean she's the right fit for your job. As we discussed at the start: there are many different applications for what we do. Because of that, agencies and practitioners develop specialties aligned with those specific needs.

For example, some agencies focus entirely on corporate messaging, others on marketing and branding. There are others that only work with politicians, or law firms, or banks. Choose a team that has the right expertise.

How do you do that? Make it a priority to learn as much as possible about the people you're meeting and ask a lot of questions. Always keep in mind that no one knows your business or your needs as well as you do. Take the time to gather specifics about what each potential partner can do to help you reach your goals.

Dear PR Pro:

My team is clear on our marketing, and we know the benefits of PR, but we're a small company. Can we really afford this?

—BUDGET CONSCIOUS

Dear Budget Conscious:

There are many ways to do PR, including options that fit even the smallest budgets. If you really need to start small, take that marketing plan and decide which piece will benefit most from a PR program. Even if you choose to promote a single product, service, or person, take time to identify why that is the right one and what the optimal end result of PR will be. Having clarity on the goal will help you decide how much to spend.

Now that you know the size and scope of the PR project, you're ready to look for the best partner. Is your initiative small enough that a PR person can manage it in a few hours per week? Then you might want to consider hiring a freelancer whose time you can limit to only what is needed. Maybe it's a little bigger than that and you want different experts working at the same time. No problem. Add a second freelancer with a different background, or bring on a small agency that has a range of talent on their team along with flexible budget arrangements.

Maybe, after considering all that you need to get accomplished, you will decide to partner with a larger agency. Make sure to find one with the right team for your business.

To help you make these budgeting decisions, please download our free PR Budget Quiz at lightspeedpr.com/resources. It's an easy tool for understanding the level of PR you can afford along with helpful insights that will help you make the most of that budget.

Of course, after all the work you've done, you'll be thrilled to start working with your new PR partner. Remember not to jump in without paying close attention to your Statement of Work, commonly referred to as an SOW.* This document will guide your team and should be as detailed as possible.

I warned you in my Introduction that PR people love acronyms. Use the Glossary at the end of the book for a complete list of the ones I've covered here.

 Dear PR Pro:

Do I have to hire a dedicated PR person? I already have someone on my staff with PR experience. Can't I just give this work to them?
—OTHER OPTIONS

Dear Other Options:

I hear this question a lot. I typically answer that having an internal resource for PR is a great way to go, but with a big watch-out.

Don't forget that your staff person was hired for another job that they are currently busy doing. If you can find a way to free up their time to also do PR, fantastic. If you can't, then your PR initiative might not get the attention it needs.

This is also a good opportunity to remind you of what I said earlier: not all PR people are the same. Find out if your employee's PR background includes the right type of experience for what you're looking to do. For example, do they know how to write an effective press release and contact your business's target reporters? Or was their experience in something else that might not translate as well to your current needs?

It's possible that your employee should be the one who manages a public relations freelancer or agency. No matter what you end up deciding, start by understanding what your team can realistically do.

Dear PR Pro:

Even low-budget options are more than I want to spend. I don't have a PR expert on my team but, c'mon, anyone can write a press release and put it on the wire, right?

—I GOT THIS

Dear I Got This:

You're right, anyone can write a press release and put it on the wire. Unfortunately, without the right planning and follow-up, that press release is unlikely to achieve much for your business. And since you're concerned about spending, I should warn you: wire services can cost hundreds, or even thousands, of dollars.

Let me tell you another story about a client who spent a great deal of money on a wire service subscription. They used it to post the occasional press release that was then added to the Newsroom section on their website.

When we came on board, we asked for an audit of those efforts. That's when they discovered that the press releases hadn't earned them any SEO (search engine optimization) or new customers. Worse, awareness of their product was exactly the same as it had been before they started, and their website's Newsroom had zero visitors.

As you can imagine, they weren't happy to learn that. They came to the same realization as most of our clients who go this route: impactful PR requires more than just posting press releases.

Let's go back to that gym analogy we spoke about earlier. Anyone can buy a membership to their local gym. But if they never go inside, or they stop in occasionally without knowing how to use any of the equipment, it will be almost impossible for them to increase their fitness levels. (Unless the gym is really far from their home and they run there, I suppose.)

My point is, if you want to make something worthwhile, you have to do it right.

We've talked in previous chapters about how gaining media coverage requires a lot of key steps, many of which happen before writing a press release. I've also detailed the importance of doing the right kind of work after sending the release. If you skip these steps, you will more than likely waste money on the wire distribution of a press release that no one sees.

I'm glad you brought this up, I Got This. Being careful to plan your budget against the right resources is a good way to get started. But that's only one element of your PR program that requires close attention. I would be remiss if I didn't share some other warnings from my many years of experience with clients who ended up disappointed because they approached PR in the wrong way.

Join me in Chapter 7.

> To help you make these budgeting decisions, please download our free **PR Budget Quiz** at lightspeedpr.com/resources. It's an easy tool for understanding the level of PR you can afford along with helpful insights that will help you make the most of that budget.

CHAPTER **07**

OPTIMIZING YOUR SYSTEM

 Dear PR Pro:
I'm doing everything you said to find the right PR team. Once they're hired, I can step away and let them achieve my goals, right?
—SET IT AND FORGET IT

Dear Set It and Forget It:
Sadly, that is wrong. Think about other investments in your business and your life. Do you hire employees and then ignore them? Or do you manage their work and oversee their progress?

How about a car or a house you might own. Do you watch out for issues and intervene when necessary? I hope you said yes to all of the above. (Don't worry if you never clean behind the refrigerator. No one does that.)

While your PR team is likely a capable group of people with the right background and skills, they can't work in a vacuum.

Maybe it's time for another story. Years ago, my agency worked for a wonderful company that was growing fast. They knew they could do even better by adding a PR program, so they took their time to get to know our team, agreed we were the right fit, and then hired us. Unfortunately, we could almost never get their attention after that.

My team did everything we could to set the stage for press outreach: we developed a PR plan, researched their competitors, created lists of target media, and even spoke to some of their customers. Every time we asked the client to help us develop the story that would drive news coverage, they never had time. Despite asking repeatedly for more details about the customers we had met, we got no answer. Our media leads shared feedback from reporters that the company's website was difficult to use, and their messaging unclear. Nothing changed. We even ghost-wrote some articles on their behalf that their internal team never got around to approving.

On the few occasions we did get their attention, it was only for a few minutes at a time, which they generally used to tell us to "just figure it out."

Unfortunately, that couldn't work. No matter how much information you share with your PR team, they can't possibly know your business as well as you do. In the case of this partnership, that meant we were never able to uncover the right ways to talk about them to the media.

I'm sorry to say they spent a lot of money on a PR program that only accomplished a small amount of what would have been possible with the right level of attention from their side.

As a rule, we require our clients to dedicate four hours per week to working with us. With any less than that, neither team is in a position to achieve their goals.

Dear PR Pro:

Our story is easy to understand, it's all about the great work we do for our own customers.

—CHECK US OUT

Dear Check Us Out:

My team often works with businesses whose story is built around the work they do for others, like you. Often, we're able to gain lots of awareness on their behalf. Other times, however, we face an insurmountable obstacle.

Building press outreach entirely on the work you do for someone else presents another problem: you have to get permission to tell the story. Sometimes your customers are happy to agree. After all, they earn free PR in the process. Other times, sadly, they are not on board.

Maybe they work in a closely regulated industry. Or, they have competitors who are always looking for inside information. Many companies are careful to control any news reported on them with their own PR teams. Whatever the reason, it's smart to get approval to tell another business's story before you hire PR.

Which reminds me, the clients I've named in this book have given permission to be mentioned here. Except Blarg, of course. Reaching hypothetical business leaders is notoriously difficult to do.

 Dear PR Pro:

My story is not based on my company's work. We have innovative and groundbreaking things happening within our own business, and I'm certain we're ready to tell the world.

—FOLLOW MY LEAD

Dear Follow My Lead:

Sounds exciting! Before you go too far down the road with PR, I implore you to make sure that everyone else in your company agrees. Because if your leadership is not ready to "tell the world," that can cause big problems for your PR team. And, maybe, you.

My agency has learned this the hard way. Those experiences usually involved a client lead who was an excellent marketing manager, or another internal communications leader, who rightly believed it was time to gain public awareness for their company's work.

In one case, we developed a great PR program only to discover that the company's CEO was nervous that their tech wasn't ready for launch. Everything we did was scrapped.

Another time we had a company leader decide that the story we believed was their strongest for media coverage wasn't the one he wanted to tell. In short order, he undid all our work and insisted on a new direction that ultimately failed. (Another instance where someone misunderstanding PR led to problems. I wish we could have given him this book!)

Other examples include CEOs who are too introverted to do media interviews; are concerned about revealing too much about their business; or have been burned by a negative news report in the past. I'm sorry to report that I've experienced all of these situations. And every one of them had the potential to ruin a lot of great work done by my agency, as well as the client's own employees who were managing us.

While you and your team might have great vision for your company's messaging, and all the right elements in place for outstanding PR results, without the buy-in of senior leadership it will be hard to realize any of it.

For more on what can go wrong when starting a PR program, and to take a quiz to see if you're ready, download our free, step-by-step article **Where PR Goes Wrong, and How to Make Sure it Doesn't Happen to You** at lightspeedpr.com/resources.

Dear PR Pro:

My leadership is just as excited as I am. They have a lot of business goals for this quarter that we want to achieve through PR.

—READY FOR RESULTS

Dear Ready for Results:

Happy to hear you have all the necessary support from your leaders. Now, did you build in enough time? As I've said before, PR is most valuable because it's earned. It needs a lot of planning and development to get to where you want to go. Sometimes that happens quickly, but more often than not, it takes time.

In other words, leveraging PR to reach your business goals is an excellent plan. But it's unrealistic to expect those goals to be achieved within the current quarter.

In fact, one of the most common reasons PR doesn't work as well as expected is because the team wasn't given enough lead time. Far too frequently a partner tells us they have a new product launch happening in a few weeks, or big news popping on Monday. At that point, it's far too late to give PR enough runway for the planning, implementation, and follow-up required to gain any real results.

My best advice is to start thinking about promotions at the same time you're developing whatever it is you believe is worthy of news. No doubt, that new product or service you're pushing out into the world spent a lot of time in development. Or perhaps you're announcing a senior hire or a big shift in the way your company does business. Those things all take time to come together, so incorporate your PR planning during the developmental phases too. Any later might be too late.

So, you've done all the right planning, built in plenty of time, and have all your needed permissions as well as buy-in from senior leadership. Most importantly, you have something to share publicly that fits into one or more of the three I's: Innovation, Impact, Insight. That means you have a great story and all the right pieces in place to tell it.

What happens next?

> For more on what can go wrong when starting a PR program, and to take a quiz to see if you're ready, download our free, step-by-step article **Where PR Goes Wrong, and How to Make Sure it Doesn't Happen to You** at lightspeedpr.com/resources.

CHAPTER **08**

ENJOYING YOUR SYSTEM

 Dear PR Pro:
I've followed all of your advice, hired a great PR partner, and gave them everything they needed to do the job well. What can I expect now?

—REAP THE REWARDS

Dear Reap the Rewards:
Congratulations! It's exciting to bring on a PR partner and start exploring all that can be accomplished together. You're probably anxious to see the results start rolling in, and also to justify the budget you've allocated for this team. Let's take a quick look at what will likely happen next.

First, I absolutely have to remind you about our conversation on timing. Good public relations grows from strategy, planning, story development and, of course, outreach to reporters and other audiences. Make sure to give your team all the lead time to do these things well.

Another reminder: the PR team needs access to you and your team. The better your PR partners can learn about such facts as your business goals, subject matter expertise, products, services, leadership, industry events, and competitors, the better they can function as a valuable partner to you. So, spend some time with them.

What happens once that time is invested and your team really starts working for you? Let's imagine you own Blarg, Inc. (our favorite fictitious client), and you're about to launch the delightful product, Widget. Remember all the PR elements we put into place for this? Here's a quick review:

- Developed a media strategy and key messaging based on their marketing research and other discovery sessions with the team.

- Secured a presence at consumer events.

- Earned prestigious industry awards.

- Placed the CEO as a keynote speaker at a leadership conference.

- Developed an investor relations program.

- Built out a media relations program based on competitive research and audience targeting.

- Developed press releases, pitches, contributed articles, and other content to engage with target media for coverage.

What happens now?

Your PR team and your internal team should keep a close eye on indicators for results and start to track how they change after your program has been implemented. Ask yourself: Are you seeing an increase in sales? Are your social media channels getting more engagement? Are your company leaders being sought out by the press for expert commentary? Are you attracting more investors, partners, employees?

Your PR team will also give you regular reports that include measurements such as:

- **Media coverage:** the news articles they have secured for you.

- **Total impressions:** the estimated number of people reached by that coverage.

- **Share of Voice:** how you compare to your competitors in the industry.

- **Unique Visitors Monthly:** the number of visitors to your website.

- **Advertising Value (AVE):** the cost of running an advertisement in the same publication where your articles appeared.

> - Media coverage
> - Total impressions
> - Share of Voice
> - Unique Visitors Monthly
> - Advertising Value (AVE)

At all times, both your internal team and your PR team should track progress against your Key Performance Indicators (KPIs). If you keep your goals for public relations clear and top of mind, it's easier to stay focused on achieving them.

 Dear PR Pro:

I'm sure that our initial round of activities is going to be successful. What happens after that first press release is done?

—NOW WHAT

Dear Now What:

I'm sure your company has goals to achieve beyond the first announcement. Your PR team can help you develop creative and insightful ways to continue reaching your business's KPIs.

For example, maybe you want reporters to experience your product by sending them samples or through a press event. Perhaps your CEO has emerged as a leading voice for your industry and there are even more opportunities to develop them as a thought leader. A strategic PR team will also be thinking of new ways to reach your audience, maybe through regional media or targeted events at places like schools, shopping malls, offices, or—if you're Blarg—movie theaters.

Once your business starts generating awareness, no doubt you will have an impact story to share with the media. Your PR team can work with you to craft a message around the ways in which your company, product, or service has changed or improved your industry overall.

Let's not forget about your internal company news either: announce new hires, significant growth, acquisitions of other businesses, expansion into new markets, and other noteworthy updates. There are always new and different ways to keep your business top of mind for the media and your target audiences.

 ### Dear PR Pro:

Sure, I get all of that. But honestly, is it all really worth it?

—WANT TO BELIEVE

Dear Want to Believe:

If you've done your preparation and partnered with good practitioners, then I'm happy to say yes, it is worth it. So far, I've shared stories about work that didn't go well. Let me give you a few examples of when it did.

Remember the medical device client that my team at Lightspeed PR/M represented? Back in Chapter 4, I shared that, in this particular instance, we realized we had to start our outreach with targeted reporters at scientific publications.

Our strategy paid off. With that critical first step achieved, we were able to steadily build our press outreach to higher and higher tiered publications. Within a few months, our remarkable client was no longer a brief mention in articles about their technology—they were the headline. In fact, within the first year of our partnership, they gained coverage in more than 115 articles, podcasts, and news programs, with a total audience of over 4.5 billion.

Other indicators showed the results of our PR program too. For example, their Twitter profile visits soared, while on LinkedIn we doubled the company's following in just six months. Website traffic driven from LinkedIn also increased over 1,000 percent in that same time period.

And remember that robot company I mentioned in Chapter 5? After our initial learning period, we shifted away from technology adopters and had overwhelming success. By focusing on the real-life users of the robot and the company's partnerships with hospitals, schools, and even sports teams, we earned a wide range of media coverage demonstrating its life-changing applications. Before long, our refreshed PR program secured more than 385 million placements for this extraordinary company, with a total audience reach of over 3.2 billion impressions.

As for those other metrics that can result from PR? This particular client reported that sales of their robot solutions skyrocketed as a result of our press coverage.

Of course, two examples barely scratch the surface. In my three decades working in PR, I've seen stunning turnarounds after companies deploy public relations to achieve their goals. PR can be applied to sell products or services, influence political leaders, attract investors, support employees, manage a crisis, educate, influence, and refocus. Which is to say, if it's not part of your marketing plan, it is certainly worth considering.

You might also find you get a lot more from your partnership with a PR expert than expected. Speaking generally, we're a lively group. The profession tends to attract creative types who have a passion for interacting with people. On many occasions I've had a friend, or a client—sometimes even a stranger—tell me that I connect well with people, and I have a knack for saying things in a way that makes others sit up and take interest. I'm delighted to hear such comments because working with people is what I love. But my response is always the same: "That's my job."

ENDNOTES

1 Nearly 180 Million Shop Over Thanksgiving Holiday Weekend, National Retail Federation, Nov 30, 2021 (https://nrf.com/media-center/press-releases/nearly-180-million-shop-over-thanksgiving-holiday-weekend)

2 Small Business Saturday Statistics in 2022, Bankrate, Nov 21, 2022

3 The Phrase that Put Peoria on the Map, Peoria Magazine, https://www.peoriamagazine.com/archive/ibi_article/2009/phrase-put-peoria-map/.

4 Knight, Jerry, Tylenol's Maker Shows How to Respond to Crisis, Washington Post, Oct 11, 1982, (https://www.washingtonpost.com/archive/business/1982/10/11/tylenols-maker-shows-how-to-respond-to-crisis/bc8df898-3fcf-443f-bc2f-e6fbd639a5a3/)

PUBLIC RELATIONS GLOSSARY OF TERMS

Angle / Hook
The "so what?" part of any pitch or PR tactic. This informs the messaging/approach used to communicate about the company or current event. Should answer: why this is interesting/noteworthy/why audiences should care.

Award submission
In order to win a company award (e.g. Top Workplace, TIME100) company representatives/PR professionals fill out an application (and often pay a fee) that enters them into eligibility.

Brand
Brand has two meanings in business:
1. (literal) A product or service manufactured and sold under a certain name.
2. (figurative) The identity or personality associated with a company which is the result of the brand's tone, mission, values, and actions.

Briefing document
Includes details about an upcoming interview, e.g., the outlet, journalist, and potential questions/talking points.

Byline / Contributed content
An article written by (i.e., bylined by) a company spokesperson as a contributor to the outlet where the piece is published.

Case study
An in-depth look at a specific event or customer/client experience. Case Studies offer an opportunity to learn more about a company through a real-world example.

Crisis communication
The specific, reactive communication strategy employed when addressing a crisis.

Earned media
Media coverage that is free. Not an advertisement.

Embargoed
Information shared in secrecy. Not to be shared before a certain date and time (typically the same time as official company announcement).

Exclusive
Offering one outlet the opportunity to be the first to run coverage of the announcement exclusively, for a predetermined window of time.

Fact-checking
Verifying the accuracy of any given piece of content (e.g., article, press release).

Headline
The title of an article.

Impression
The number of people who could have watched/read/encountered content.

Marketing plan
A road map that the marketing team follows and implements to reach its goals.

Media list
List of journalists with something in common (e.g., beat or location).

Media monitoring
Combing media regularly for relevant information to be gathered and used in reports. Typically includes company mentions, competitor mentions, and industry news/trends.

Media training
Training session(s) for company spokespeople to prepare them for media opportunities. Sessions typically cover how to manage a conversation with a journalist to deliver the messages of the spokesperson.

Mission statement
A one- or two-sentence declaration of a company's ultimate purpose.

Newswire
A press release distribution service that generates automatic pickup of a press release across a range of predetermined outlets. While customer service representatives may assist with uploading a release, the distribution happens via computer automation.

Paid media
Any media that is the result of money exchanged for coverage/publication.

Pay-to-play
Opportunities for publication through purchase.

PR vs. Publicity vs. Propaganda

Public Relations: Managing public perception of an organization by creating the right kind of awareness and driving action to achieve business goals.

Publicity: Garnering public awareness of any kind.

Propaganda: The dissemination of biased information with the aim of persuading audiences for (usually political) gain.

Press kit

A prepackaged set of materials about a company provided as background information to the press. This might include logos, boilerplates, and spokesperson headshots/bios.

Press release

An official statement released by a company.

Public relations

Managing public perception of an organization by creating the right kind of awareness and driving action to achieve business goals.

Stakeholder

An individual with an interest in a company, (e.g., employees, investors, customers, business partners). Stakeholders care about, or will be affected by, the company and its news/developments.

Subhead

A line below the headline of an article. This is often longer than the headline and provides more context. Note: Not all articles have a subhead.

Style Guide

A document detailing how one should write/speak/design about a company.

Speaking submission
Similar to an award submission, but typically without the fee. A speaking submission is required for consideration to speak at an event.

Spokesperson
A representative of a company/organization. Generally, the term is not used for thought leader/subject matter expert. Rather, a spokesperson makes announcements or comments on behalf of the company.

Target audience
The group of people to whom a message is aimed. This group varies depending on the message and is decided based on the strategy or on data.

Thought leader
An expert who provides valuable insight to contribute to an ongoing conversation, publicly establishing them or the company as knowledgeable.

Tiers of publications
Top Tier media outlets (sometimes called A-list): The most prestigious and held in the highest regard, with some of the largest (national) audiences.

Tier 2 media: More specific than top tier, with a slightly smaller but still substantial reach to the target audience. Highly regarded in specific areas or industry.

Tier 3 media: Local or industry-specific blogs relevant to the target audience.

Tier 4 media: Less relevant to the audience, or small but relevant bloggers or publications.

Trendjacking
Identifying relevant current events in media that can be leveraged for media coverage.

Whitepaper
A document published by a company that contains data and information/analysis.

PUBLIC RELATIONS ACRONYMS

B2B Business to Business. B2B companies partner with or sell to other businesses.

B2C Business to Consumer/Customer. B2C companies sell directly to private consumers.

CPC Cost Per Click, used for advertisement purchases. CPC ads are only charged in the event that a user clicks on the ad.

KPI Key Performance Indicator. KPIs are the metrics/data points that reflect the success (or lack thereof) of certain efforts. Common KPIs include: number of placements per month, number of clicks, number of signups or form-fills.

RFP Request for Proposal. Often used by a business to request a formal proposal of services from suppliers (e.g., PR agencies).

ROAS Return on Advertising Spend. This is a more specific way of expressing "return on investment (ROI)" but the investment in question is specific to advertising spend. ROAS is calculated by the ad platform being used based on how much it costs to run the ad vs. the resulting sales revenue.

SEO   Search Engine Optimization. Intentionally designing websites and website copy to be optimized for searching, thus moving the webpages up in the search engine's relevancy ranking and driving more traffic to the site. Some elements of SEO include: relevant keywords, credible links within the site, and consistently functional landing pages.

SME   Subject Matter Expert. A person who has expertise regarding a selected subject(s). It is used to replace the general term "expert."

SOV   Share of Voice. SOV measures the amount of communication materials/media coverage from one company in a vertical comparison to relevant competitors. Measures how well ads, social media content, media coverage, and website traffic are performing compared to competitors.

SOW   Scope of Work. An overview of the work (usually including tasks and KPIs) that the agency and client have agreed to.

USP   Unique Selling Point. A measurement of how a company is distinct relative to competitors. While a USP is specific to an offering, it could be an overarching fact about a company (e.g., philanthropy).

UVP   Unique Value Proposition. A factor about a company that is compelling to its target group (e.g., consumers, partners, other businesses).

UVM   Unique Visitors Monthly. The average number of individual users visiting a website. Note: The UVM does not measure the number of times a person visits a page or website, which is a more general traffic metric. Instead, the UVM reflects how many people will likely visit the site during a month. If a person visits the site every day, they are still only counted as one visitor.

ABOUT THE AUTHOR

Amanda Proscia is the co-founder of Lightspeed Public Relations and Marketing, a New York City-based agency focused on the technology sector. Before starting Lightspeed in 2013, Amanda spent decades learning the intricacies of PR by working in a variety of other agencies, spanning from the very large ones to the very small. She also took on diverse roles, including marketing, political, corporate, non-profit, and financial public relations. After five years on the communications team at American Express, Amanda knew enough about typical PR agencies to want to build a new version. One that puts the clients, and their needs, first.

An unexpected part of her experience over the years has been fielding thousands of questions about public relations. Many of them come from business leaders who would benefit from a PR program of their own, if they just understood what it is.

Amanda's writing has been published in many top-tier publications, but—true to her profession—always under someone else's name. She has served as a ghostwriter for Fortune 50 executives, prominent politicians, and countless client leaders, helping to amplify their voices from behind the scenes.

With *PR Confidential*, she's stepping out of the shadows to make her insider's knowledge available to everyone. Find her at www.lightspeedpr.com

Printed in the USA
CPSIA information can be obtained
at www.ICGtesting.com
JSHW071914020624
64101JS00006B/14